Fulton Books, Inc.
Meadville, PA

•

Published by Fulton Books 2021

•

ISBN 978-1-64952-572-7 (Hardcover)

ISBN 978-1-64952-573-4 (Digital)

•

Printed in the
United States of America

•

•

FIRST EDITION

The Secret in the Clouds

by Ron Sachs and Gay Webster-Sachs
Illustrated & Designed by Nancy and Aurelio Sica

"Grieving people want and need to be heard, not fixed."
THE GRIEF RECOVERY METHOD

Dedication

This is for all of the children -
and for the happy child in all of us -
whose sights ought to always be uplifted with hope,
imagination, love, beauty, inspiration, and faith
in today and tomorrow.
And this story and my life are dedicated
to my pride-and-joy daughters-
Samantha Jane Sachs, Aimee Nicole Sachs,
and Julie Sachs Hunter.
You have given my life more purpose and meaning
than I ever could have dreamed.

With my love,

ACKNOWLEDGEMENTS

We salute all of the first responders and medical professionals
whose lives are devoted to protecting and caring for others.
And to the other valiant soldiers in the fight against
COVID-19:
...the people who staff nursing homes, grocery stores,
pharmacies, and every business that sought to endure and help
provide for others during the most difficult
and prolonged era of our lifetimes.

Meet The Authors & Artist

Ron Sachs

Is one of America's most experienced and respected communications consultants. He is Founder and CEO of Florida-based Sachs Media, a nationally ranked and recognized fully integrated marketing and communications firm engaged in public relations, public affairs, crisis management, research, web, video production, graphic design, and digital media. An award-winning former newspaper reporter, magazine editor, and television commentator, Ron has also served as senior communications counsel to two Governors of Florida. He is married to Gay Webster-Sachs and is father to daughters Samantha, Aimee & Julie.

Gay Webster-Sachs, LMHC

Is a Licensed Mental Health Counselor currently practicing in Tallahassee, Florida. A former teacher, her professional career included work at Hospice Of Southeast Florida, helping patients, families, and children. She has specialized in providing individual and group therapy for children, helping them understand the death and dying process and how to cope with loss and grief. Gay also worked for Nova Southeastern University's Center for Psychological Studies as a rehabilitation therapist and treatment specialist with chronically mentally ill geriatric patients.

Nancy Simons Sica

Is a Graduate of the University of Florida with a Degree in Advertising and Design. Nancy is an Award-Winning Art Director, Designer and Children's Book Illustrator at Miami's Aurelio & Friends Advertising. She is Executive Vice-President and business partner with her husband, Aurelio. They are very proud of their three accomplished daughters...Vanessa, an Industrial Designer, Amanda, a Graphic Designer and Victoria, a Corporate Attorney, as well as grandparents of...*Two* sets of adorable *Twins*, Aero & Valentina, Hazel & Sparrow and the newest addition to their family, granddaughter Vera Grace.

Sunny Albright was a happy, smart, and creative girl. She loved her family, school, friends, playing, art – and all her life.

At school, she was a good student – quick to answer her teacher's questions. At play with friends, she was always the first to see amazing pictures of animals, boats, flowers, and people forming in the clouds.

At home, Sunny loved being with her Mom and Dad, her little brother Andy, who was only three, and their fun dog, Buddy.

She helped with chores and always looked forward to their family time.

ne night, Sunny saw her parents look more worried than she had ever seen them before, as they watched the news on TV. It was all about a **'global pandemic'** from a virus called **COVID-19**.

The news was about how this virus was making lots of people sick, all over the world – and how some were also dying from it. And now, the virus was in the United States, too! Sunny knew from her parents' serious reaction that this was a sad, bad thing that was going to affect everyone.

Sunny heard her parents discuss what to do to protect the family, including Sunny's Grandma Hope, who lived in a nearby assisted living home for older people. The news said older people were especially in danger of getting the virus, so they wanted to be sure she would be as safe as possible.

Sunny liked to visit with Grandma Hope – who always sang songs to her, told her interesting stories about her own childhood, and shared what Sunny's Mom was like as a little girl. Soon, the concern about the spread of the dangerous virus changed everything in Sunny's life – and for all of her family, friends, and community, too.

Everyone was staying home from school, work, church, parks, parties, and shops. This was all at the direction of government and health leaders, to try to stop the virus from spreading.

Sunny and her family couldn't even visit their Grandma Hope nearby – because to protect older people, visits were not allowed during this virus danger. So, they talked to Grandma Hope by phone every day.

At first, Sunny and her little brother enjoyed the break from their normal routine. Staying at home, they did art projects, played in the backyard, watched TV, and loved the extra time with their Mom and Dad and their frisky dog, Buddy.

But after a little while, it was boring to just stay at home all of the time.

Sunny's parents told her there had never been a time as tough as this in their lives. She could feel how worried they were by their whispered voices and serious looks, every day.

Then they explained to Sunny that her Grandma Hope had become very sick from the virus. She was too sick to even speak on the phone. She had been taken to an isolation room, so that other people would not be exposed to the virus. This news made Sunny very sad and worried.

She and her family prayed for Grandma Hope to recover.

*A*s days turned into weeks, Sunny began to lose her spirit and brightness.

She didn't look up at the clouds much now, and when she did, she didn't see any pictures of anything. She was very tired of this major change in her life. She was missing Grandma Hope. Now, this long stay-at-home wasn't fun at all – it just made her sad.

The TV news every night talked about more people getting sick – and more people dying. And just when it seemed it couldn't get worse, it did.

Sunny's parents sat down with her in the living room and explained that Grandma Hope's sickness had caused her to die.

Sunny collapsed in tears and she had never, ever been sadder.

She never got to see Grandma Hope for a last visit, to talk, hug, kiss or say a final goodbye. Sunny's parents knew that she needed help to cope with the sadness of losing her beloved Grandma.

So, Sunny's parents set up an online video chat for her to talk with a professional grief counselor, Ms. Webster -- a smart and kind woman who was experienced at helping people express their feelings about losing a loved one.

Sunny cried as she described her hurt about the sadness of losing Grandma Hope.

She talked about how hard it was to stay at home for so long without getting to be with her classmates, neighborhood friends and the normal life they could no longer enjoy.

Just talking to this counselor made Sunny feel a little better. Ms. Webster said things that helped Sunny understand that dying is a part of living, for all people and creatures.

Sunny's parents told her they would schedule more talks for Sunny with Ms. Webster, the helpful counselor.

That night, as Sunny slept,
a gentle force from the heavens
visited her room and carefully
and kindly lifted her imagination
from her sleeping mind.
Sunny's imagination
looked just like her!

When Sunny
opened her eyes
after her magical trip skyward,
she was surprised at what she saw.

She was safely standing on
top of a cluster of fluffy clouds,
surrounded by sweet-looking
little cloudlike creatures who
all smiled at her.

**"Where am I?
And who are you?"**
Sunny asked with wonder,
and without any fear.

One of the cloud creatures
smiled and answered her,
**"Welcome, Sunny.
We are the Cloud People.**

We have brought you
here to help you feel better.
We want to share a
special secret with you, it's...
The Secret in the Clouds."

Sunny lit up with excitement,
as she enjoyed this very special
place with all of the Cloud People.

13

Wisp

Cumulo

*O*ne by one,
the cloudlike faces
told Sunny their names...

**Wisp...Cumulo...Puffy...
Cirrus...Cloudette...Nimbus
...Stratus and Splash!**

They were all so nice –
like new friends.

They explained that they
each represented a type of
cloud that appears in the sky –
and that they quietly and
very secretly worked up
there in the skies.

Puffy

Cirrus

Cloudette

"We make pictures in the clouds so that you and all of the people on earth can be delighted, just by looking upward and seeing nice things," Nimbus explained.

"I've always enjoyed seeing pictures in the clouds of animals, shapes, flowers, even people," Sunny replied, with a bit of glee.

Then Stratus explained more, "We are sort of like the elves who work for Santa – except we are the special workers for the angels.
They give us the power and energy to make the pretty pictures because most clouds are really the artwork of the angels."

Sunny could hardly contain her excitement.
"Tell me more, please. I love pretty clouds and the pictures in them."

"Well," said Stratus. "On a cloudy day, we are hard at work making nice pictures for people to see, to cheer them up from their troubles."

"On a clear day, we have the day off!
And the reason people see so many puppies and dogs in the cloud pictures is because it really is true -- that 'all dogs go to heaven.' Really."
Sunny was delighted.

15

Nimbus

Stratus

"What about those scary thunder-storms, with dark clouds, thunder and lightning?" she asked.

Splash laughed and replied, "Oh, that's just nature making sure there's enough rain for all living things."

Splash

Then, Sunny's new Cloud Friends surrounded her and whispered to her that she could have the power and energy to make pictures in the clouds, too, by just imagining whatever she wanted to see.

"Really? I can do that now?" Sunny asked.

"You've always had the power – and so do most people," explained Wisp.

"But they're too busy to slow down, relax, and look up to imagine and see all of the beauty around them and the wonders we are creating. But when they do, wonderful pictures appear."

So, Sunny closed her eyes,
while her Cloud Friends urged
her on, and she imagined
a picture of a beautiful rainbow
and a Unicorn. When she opened
her eyes, there it was in the clouds,
just as she had imagined it.

"It's my Lucky Unicorn!"
Sunny said, laughing.

**"Now that you know The Secret in the Clouds,
you can go home and use your belief and energy
to be a Cloud Angel on earth – imagining pictures
to cheer up everybody, just like we do,"** said Stratus.

**"And, if you want to, you can teach others how to
do it by sharing The Secret in the Clouds with them."**

$\mathcal{S}$unny thanked her new friends, hugged them all goodbye – and then, just as magically as her imagination had been whisked skyward, it was safely returned back to her sleeping self, at home, on earth.

When Sunny awoke the next morning, she was full of energy and the kind of joy she used to feel, before the virus caused people to stay at home. She hugged her parents and little brother, Andy, and told them...

"I can't wait to see what good things happen today."

Sunny's parents explained that their town was going to start **'safely reopening'** – and they could carefully go back to parks, stores, church, restaurants, and life the way it used to be.

Then, the family took a little trip to a nearby park. They wore masks and kept a safe distance from other people

$\mathcal{S}$ unny was excited about seeing her friends again and returning to school when it started back up, after the long shutdown. Her Mom and Dad were going to be able to go back to their jobs – and Andy, back to pre-school.

Then Sunny asked them all to lay down in the grass, side by side, and look up to the clouds in the sky.

Sunny closed her eyes for a few seconds and imagined the cloud picture she wanted to create for her family to see. When she opened her eyes, she pointed to a cluster of clouds that were moving and forming a new shape.

*S*unny's Mom and Dad both gasped with surprise, while Sunny smiled as she pointed directly to the image that she wanted her brother Andy to see, too.

"Do you see?" she asked.

"Look at Grandma Hope – smiling down at us. She looks so peaceful and happy, doesn't she?"

*T*ears of happiness filled their eyes,
as they stood up to watch Grandma
Hope's sweet face float across the sky,
before disappearing into some larger clouds.

They all embraced in a loving family hug.
Sunny had a big announcement to make to her family.

"Last night in my dreams, I learned about...

THE SECRET IN THE CLOUDS

**It's really all about just believing in good things,
being grateful and seeing the beauty
in each and every day."**

There are 3 Main Cloud Types. CIRRUS • CUMULUS • STRATUS. These Names can be

HIGH ALTITUDE CLOUDS   UP To 50,000 Ft

Cirrus
Cirrocumulus
Cumulonimbus
Cirrostratus

Clouds that produce precipitation often have
names containing the word part 'Nimbo' or 'Nimbus'

Cirrus

36,000 ft

MEDIUM ALTITUDE CLOUDS   UP To 20,000 Ft

Altocumulus
Altostratus

Clouds that form at a medium altitude
have names with the Pre-fix 'Alto'

Altocumulus

LOW ALTITUDE CLOUDS   From Ground Up To 6,500 Ft

Cumulus
Stratus
Nimbostratus

5,000 ft

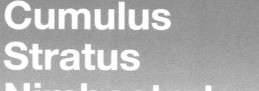

Cloud Chart

ombined with each other, and with other word parts to identify more specific Cloud types.

Cirrocumulus

Cirrostratus

Altostratus

Cumulonimbus

Nimbostratus

Cumulus

Stratus

Helpful Mental Health Resources
for Children and Families

The outbreak of Coronavirus disease 2019
(COVID-19)
may be stressful and can be overwhelming and
cause strong emotions in adults and children.
Taking care of your emotional health
will help you think clearly.

Children and Grief —— Hospice Foundation of America (hospicefoundation.org)

Grief and Loss CDC ———————————————— (www.cdc.gov)

Grief Resources, Hospice, and Community Care
———————————— (www.hospiceandcommunitycare.org › grief-links)

Helping Children Cope with Loss ———————— (www.caredimensions.org)

Helping Children Process Grief & Loss during COVID-19 —— (nyulangone.org)

Mental Health and Coping during COVID-19 CDC ———— (www.cdc.gov)

Supporting Families during COVID-19 —— **Child Mind Institute** (childmind.org)

Coping with Grief ———————————————— (store.samhsa.gov)

Grief and Children —— **Facts for Families** ———— (www.aacap.org)

Guiding Adults in Talking to Children about Death ——— (www.nctsn.org)

Helping Children Cope with Changes Resulting from COVID-19
——————————————————— (www.nasponline.org)

How to Support Kids' Mental Health during the COVID-19
———————— (www.thechildren.com › conditions-and-illnesses › how...)

Mental Health of Adolescents before and after a Death
———————————————— (www.ncbi.nlm.nih.gov)

Trauma and Grief Resources ——————— (healthinschools.org)

CPSIA information can be obtained
at www.ICGtesting.com
Printed in the USA
LVHW070809300321
682901LV00002B/5